# My Wolf

*poems by*

# Kate McNairy

*Finishing Line Press*
Georgetown, Kentucky

# My Wolf

*It is a joy to be hidden, and a disaster not to be found.*
*D.W. Winnicott*

Copyright © 2021 by Kate McNairy
ISBN 978-1-64662-548-2 First Edition
All rights reserved under International and Pan-American Copyright Conventions. No part of this book may be reproduced in any manner whatsoever without written permission from the publisher, except in the case of brief quotations embodied in critical articles and reviews.

## ACKNOWLEDGMENTS

Thank you to the following periodical for publishing my poems included in this collection:

*Raven's Perch*—"Knot Theory," "We Fill Each Other with Radiance"

Publisher: Leah Huete de Maines
Editor: Christen Kincaid
Cover Art: ArtTower via Pixaby
Author Photo: Elizabeth Macy, Image Photo & Events
Cover Design: Jon Sargalis

Order online: www.finishinglinepress.com
　　　　　also available on amazon.com

　　　　　　　　Author inquiries and mail orders:
　　　　　　　　　　　Finishing Line Press
　　　　　　　　　　　　PO Box 1626
　　　　　　　　　　　Georgetown, Kentucky 40324
　　　　　　　　　　　　　　USA

# Table of Contents

| | |
|---|---:|
| Arising | 1 |
| Losing It | 2 |
| Pink Flamingo | 3 |
| Dog Days | 4 |
| Her Coat | 5 |
| Logic | 6 |
| Gravity of the Situation | 7 |
| Our Quarrel Ends at 2:00 a.m. | 8 |
| Night Revelry | 9 |
| My Wolf | 10 |
| To a Stag | 11 |
| The Pageant | 12 |
| I Don't Know Anyone | 13 |
| July 4th | 14 |
| A Bursting Star | 15 |
| This Morning | 16 |
| In One's Element | 17 |
| Tomatoes | 18 |
| Knot Theory | 19 |
| In Redwood Forests | 20 |
| More Than Likely | 21 |
| Homecoming | 22 |
| We Fill Each Other With Radiance | 23 |
| The Price | 24 |
| South of the Border | 25 |
| How to Let Go | 26 |
| Home | 27 |
| Invisible | 28 |
| Creature Feature | 29 |
| Hospice | 30 |
| It Comes and Goes | 31 |
| Dreams | 32 |
| Befuddled | 33 |
| That Good Night | 34 |

**Arising**

After a warm showy summer night
now early morning gray veiled fog—

I wake and throw back my sheets
seduce my unquiet mind.

I draw the flowery drapes aside
thrust open my sultry window.

**Losing It**

Anxious at dawn
I have a smoke—

*what life will I live today?*

voices askew in my head
stumbling feet

I stare vacantly—
all the DSM Manual
classifications

on this alarming
exhilarating day.

**Pink Flamingo**

This morning
as every morning
I put on a naked face—
soap & water
clear lotion

I'll live a little today!

Make up my face
the color of a flamingo—

loud rosy rouge
slippery coral lipstick
crooked fuchsia eyeshadow

I stand on one leg.

**Dog Days**

I wake each day—
coffee news porch

In the heat of these dog days
I will gossip with

neighbors and the like—
pretend not to be a stranger.

**Her Coat**

                This morning she smooths her leather
gloved hands into my pockets

                      She keeps red lipstick in her purse,
      hand-washes her bras and panties

                            lunches at The Whistling Kettle
            plays Mahjong in the afternoon
has a bomb shelter

my mink collar—ample a little bit costly
                      she struggles her arms into my sleeves
      buttons me to the top

                she slings my nemesis the jacket
                              into the back seat
"Where are we going?" I needle her

                "To the dry cleaner my vixen—

                        It's time."

**Logic**

I draw a circle—
it rolls down a grassy hill.

I draw another circle
the circumference of our globe.

Amid such hoopla a hue and cry
are trillions and trillions

of constellations—
I can't draw circles anymore

they are just too relentless.

**Gravity of the Situation**

On my narrow street at night
I walk in rain or snow.

I hear god's whisper
in the deep dark—

I feel gravity flying apart.

## Our Quarrel Ends at 2:00 a.m.

only to heat
up again—
our energy

splits between
yelling & sudden
quiet—

we never get
enough as

we lie in fire
on purple sheets—

it's dark & I am
hungry.

**Night Revelry**

My craving for you dangles
in dark as I wait for you

under streetlights  waves  particles
a conclave of our night village—

& soon amid faded flowery wallpaper
we will sink into an abyss of longing—

these last lost casual hours.

**My Wolf**

At dawn as each star wanes in light
       a yellow-gem-eyed wolf cries
            beneath my bed

                               his deep feral breath—I howl back
     an ache in sun's early light
for you my wolf I touch my feet to the floor.

**To a Stag**

                                  He grazes on a grassy hillock
                beside a cluster of trees
     at twilight.

Suddenly—he bolts, smears like
              a bright, racy comet
                        in the darkening.

### The Pageant

My groomer dresses
Trixie as a tart—

silver chain necklace
patent leather boots
top hat

yellow dress
pink bow-tie
brushed fur

In the mirror
I see my dog
all assed out—

my soul my devil
a fresh bark.

**I Don't Know Anyone**

Blue-hued
stained glass
windows

whiten in
snow showers
at twilight.

The universe
an array
of stars—

I do not know the
puppet master

but I love you
stranger seated
next to me

as if you were
my friend.

## July 4th

Sparklers—
small explosions

heat up as
moon hangs low.

Summers go so fast—
Will we talk?

Call out for me—

I am your
burning star.

## A Bursting Star

      falls all over me
           collapses then blasts.

This supernova is
      radiant
      fierce
      & fast

            shines on each of my lapses—
              zeros into me.

**This Morning**

I've been longing for you
as my minutes stretch to hours—

a prism splits
early morning light.

There's so much chatter
among colors

that I am not alone—
there is so much to feel

& in a clump of orange
tiger lilies by the road

petal touches petal.

**In One's Element**

Everyone builds a home
for their brain—

a roof   walls   paint

Then a stranger
opens the door—

strikes a match.

**Tomatoes**

I saunter in heat
this dog day afternoon

& see Dad's garden of tomatoes
 clumps evenly spaced in a row

I talk like he talked
to each & everyone.

**Knot Theory**

Strings tie bales of hay,
truss a turkey.

They are vexing  susceptible
to disputes that grow

thorny  tangle into knots.
While daydreaming, I rope

my hair  my strings  into a braid
that curves down the
arc of my back.

**In Redwood Forests**

It is usual to
run into you.

Today it is unusual to
meet someone not you.

**More than Likely**

The New York subway
stops at a platform &

my brother strides off
to Tacoma

my sisters amble
to warmer climes.

It goes on and on

 until I am our mother—
 no one steps off.

**Homecoming**

It's been forty years
since we raced

that souped up
yellow Camaro.

Tonight at the Holiday Inn
reach back with

your black velvet eyes
dig deep

a small yen for me?
I'm falling all over for you.

## We Fill Each Other With Radiance

I'd like a whisky sour please—
I want to make my brain iridescent.

Make it two cherries thanks—
I will share the revelry.

**The Price**

My mind is in tatters at 12:00 a.m.
I throw on my coat  walk briskly

onto streets of dark wolves
and neighborly lamps.

An injured wolf howls  his paw
caught in a steel trap—

his voice slashes madly
in this stilled  quiet night—

the price of rummaging
through the world at midnight.

## South of the Border

In the ashtray
a smoldering cigarette
ashes burnt to the nub.

In my town south of the border
hear me
my long way out.

**How to Let Go**

I am at my wildest
when I wear no camouflage.

It's then I hear
the clear bluesy cry of planets

and spill grains of white sea salt
 that scatter

on the tile floor—
taste one—a pinch of brine.

**Home**

In twilight,
        the river runs briskly—

its lapping waves
        make so much hoopla—

no longer young,
        my body is less sure.

I am in my element at home tonight
        by water's bend.

**Invisible**

After leaves fell
limbs put on snowy overcoats—

nervous hot tea
sloshed on my saucer.

The woodstove heated—
my feet up  back flat

hidden in a chair—
a cardinal is such a loud red

& among branches
I am less than zero

a nothing  not a thing.

**Creature Feature**

It sleeps in my chair at the theater
sucks my being—

this creature deep within.
I let loose in the dark—

it eats so much of me
there is almost nothing left.

**Hospice**

In this rigmarole I tie
a white balloon to my wrist.

 My arms float abandoned
above colored sheets—

let all the noise of my long lost
go swiftly quiet as church mice.

**It Comes and Goes**

At the beginning or end of this sphere  we circle
      where our green money is burned

            while the moon  an escape hatch
    has no air, no map & no change

& we hold onto our madness tighter
        keeps us close  in check.

**Dreams**

They unearth in slumber what my days cannot bear—
          their iridescent nerves whir through my mind.

    Sometimes they eat me all up

            & in this early morning dawn my lawless dreams
                    break into a madding song.

## Befuddled

I am quite old
but I will not sob—it will get me nowhere
fast, this complaining.

My addled mind tells me to howl.

Watch, I have all my history on a disc—
I push a button  forget what's next.

**That Good Night**

A beacon
lights the
harbor

where I
wander
along
this surf.

Stars so close
I own them
forever—

please god
guide me
through

this long
lingering
amble

to my well-lit
demise.

**Kate McNairy** has also published the chapbooks *June Bug* (2014) and *Light to Light* (2016). Journal and magazine credits include *Third Wednesday, Misfits, and Raven's Perch,* among others. She was on the Editorial Board of *The Apple Tree* and was a finalist in the Blue Light Poetry Prize in 2014. Kate attended the NYS Summer Writers Institute at Skidmore, The Frost Place & Tupelo. She lives with Jon in upstate New York.

CPSIA information can be obtained
at www.ICGtesting.com
Printed in the USA
BVHW080720280721
613083BV00009B/418